SPELLING
ESSENTIALS

Plurals · Vowels and Consonants · Past Tense · Apostrophe · Spelling Rules · Syllables · Suffixes · Homophones

Written by Elizabeth P. Tucker
Published by World Teachers Press®

Published with the permission of R.I.C. Publications Pty. Ltd.

Copyright © 2001 by Didax, Inc., Rowley, MA 01969. All rights reserved.

First published by R.I.C. Publications Pty. Ltd., Perth, Western Australia. Revised by Didax Educational Resources.

Printed in the United States of America.

Order Number 2-5177
ISBN 1-58324-111-6

B C D E F 07 06 05 04

Educational Resources
395 Main Street
Rowley, MA 01969
www.worldteacherspress.com

The knowledge of a few basic spelling rules can be beneficial to everyone, regardless of their spelling ability.

Understanding the reasons for such spelling rules as: doubling consonants like "t," "s," "p," "l," "m" and "n" or dropping the final "e" before adding a suffix can help everyone improve their spelling.

Spelling is one of the most important elements of writing and everyone should strive to be as accurate as possible. This can be as easy as running your eyes over your work before passing it in and keeping a dictionary handy to check any words of which you are unsure. The more conscious you are about the accuracy of your work, the better you will become!

Contents

Overview of Spelling Rules

Overview of Spelling Rules

Spelling Rules

1. To learn how to spell, master the rules and be sure to thoroughly learn all the exceptions to the rules.

2. Divide the words into syllables and then say the word three times in syllables. When writing it, say the word in syllables again.

   For example,

   > *el/e/phant*
   > *in/for/ma/tion*
   > *in/de/pen/dence*
   > *ra/di/a/tion*

3. Make sure you have the correct pronunciation.

4. Look and say words.
   These have to be learned by repetitive drilling, such as spelling the words letter by letter.

   For example,

   > *t–h–e–i–r*   *t–h–o–r–o–u–g–h–l–y*

5. **Remember** we have to use our:
   (a) **eyes** to see and read the words;
   (b) **ears** to listen to the sounds of the letters;
   (c) **tongues** to say the words clearly in syllables; and
   (d) **brains** to think whether we have spelled the word as it sounds or whether there is a catch to it.

1. The English alphabet consists of twenty-six letters. These twenty-six letters are divided into two groups:
   (a) **five vowels** – a, e, i, o, u; and
   (b) **twenty-one consonants** – the remaining letters of the alphabet.

2. Sometimes "y" acts as a vowel. This occurs when "y" has the sound of "i" in any word.

   For example,

   | by | my | sky | fly |
   | try | trying | flying | crying |

3. In the English language, each vowel represents **two kinds of sounds**. They are a **long vowel** sound or a **short vowel** sound. The sign for a **long vowel sound** is ā, ē, ī, ō, ū.

   For example,

   cāke   hēre   pīne   nōte   tūbe

   The sign for a **short vowel sound** is ă, ĕ, ĭ, ŏ, ŭ.

   For example,

   păn   gĕt   hĭt   cŏt   cŭt

Syllables

1. Words are made up of **syllables**.

2. Every syllable contains a vowel.

3. Words may have one or more syllables.

4. Always say words in syllables when writing them.

   For example,

   kan/ga/roo   hip/po/pot/a/mus
   el/e/phant   ex/am/in/a/tion

Vowels and Consonants

Rule 1

The magic or "silent e" changes short vowel sounds into long vowel sounds.

For example,

can – cane	wag – wage
dam – dame	rob – robe
hop – hope	not – note
din – dine	pin – pine
kit – kite	hug – huge
cub – cube	tub – tube

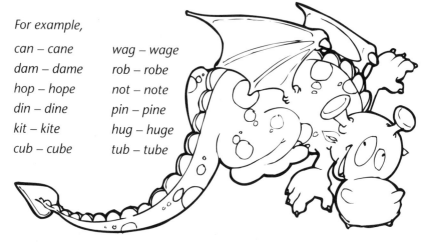

Rule 2

The consonants "f," "l" and "s" are doubled at the end of most words of one syllable.

For example,

ball	bell	bill
doll	dull	wall
off	cliff	stuff
sniff	cuff	tiff
dress	kiss	less
miss	loss	boss

Exceptions are:

of	gas	bus	was

Rule 3

"q" is generally followed by "u."

For example,

quick	quack
queen	quilt
quote	quarter
quarrel	quiz
quite	quiet
quota	quaint

 Rule 4

Both "c" and "g" have a hard and a soft sound.

a. When "c" or "g" are followed by "a," "o," or "u," they have a hard sound.

For example,

cat	cut	cap
copper	come	color
gap	got	gum
good	gone	gold

b. When "c" or "g" are followed by "e" or "i" they usually have a soft sound.

For example,

cent	civil	cycle
circle	cinema	center
gem	giant	ginger
germ	gent	

Vowels and Consonants

Rule 5

"c" and "k" sometimes have the same sound.

a. When "c" says the hard "k" sound it is generally followed by "a," "o," or "u."

For example,

cat	*can*
cut	*cannot*
cup	*cupboard*
comb	*cucumber*
carry	*camp*
company	*cubbyhouse*

b. "k" is generally followed by "e" or "i."

For example,

key	*kid*	*keep*	*kiss*
kettle	*kitten*	*kept*	*kitchen*

In a number of foreign words used in the English language and in some scientific words, "k" is followed by "a" or "o."

For example,

kaleidoscope (scientific)
kangaroo and koala (Australian Aborigine)
kowtow (Chinese)
kale (Scottish)
kapok (Malay)

✳ Rule 6

"c" and "k" go together to end a short, one-syllable word containing a short vowel.

For example,

back	neck	pick
sock	black	deck
knock	kick	truck
duck	clock	track

Exceptions are words borrowed from foreign languages.

yak (Tibetan)   amok (Malay)
kayak (Inuit)   trek (Dutch)

✳ Rule 7

"k" is always used on its own after a short vowel sound that is followed by a consonant.

For example,

pink	bank	walk
talk	think	thank
milk	silk	monkey
donkey	sank	junk

✳ Rule 8

Words are always spelled with a "k" where a double vowel precedes the "k."

For example,

speak	creek	oak	leak
week	book	spook	steak
cloak	weak	beak	look

Vowels and Consonants

☀ Rule 9

After a short vowel sound we put "d" before "ge" to keep the short vowel short.

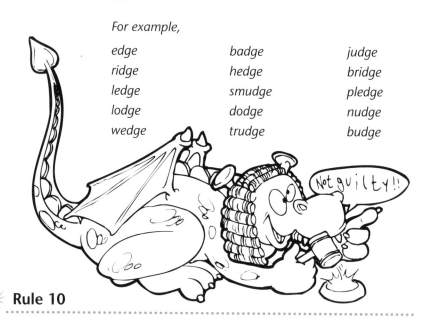

For example,

edge	*badge*	*judge*
ridge	*hedge*	*bridge*
ledge	*smudge*	*pledge*
lodge	*dodge*	*nudge*
wedge	*trudge*	*budge*

☀ Rule 10

After a short vowel sound we put "t" before "ch" to keep the short vowel short.

For example,

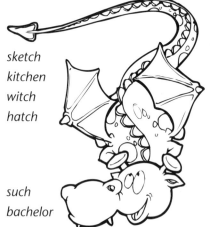

patch	*wretch*	*sketch*
match	*fetch*	*kitchen*
itch	*scratch*	*witch*
watch	*ditch*	*hatch*
catch	*latch*	

Exceptions are:

rich	*which*	*such*
much	*duchess*	*bachelor*

Rule 11

For words ending in "l" the single consonant after the short vowel has been doubled before adding "l." This is done to keep the short vowel short.

For example,

battle	muddle
puzzle	apple
nibble	bottle
peddle	kettle
middle	struggle
dazzle	giggle
wriggle	cattle
puddle	saddle

Rule 12

"s" or "z" at the end of a word is always followed by a "silent e."

For example,

horse	cause
because	house
sneeze	prize
mouse	please
geese	praise
breeze	surprise
specialize	idealize
dramatize	realize
tease	cheese
advertise	size

Vowels and Consonants

☀ Rule 13
. . . .

When the sound of "ie" says "ee" then "i" comes before "e" except after "c" when we write "ei."

a. "ie"

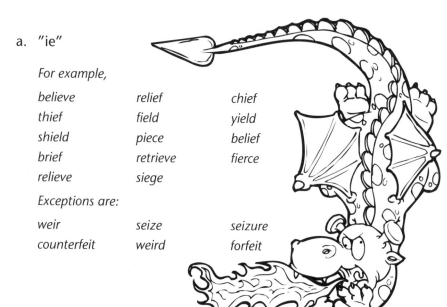

For example,

believe	relief	chief
thief	field	yield
shield	piece	belief
brief	retrieve	fierce
relieve	siege	

Exceptions are:

weir	seize	seizure
counterfeit	weird	forfeit

b. "ei" says "ee" after "c"

For example,

receive	perceive	deceit	preconceive
deceive	conceit	ceiling	conceive

c. When "ei" does not say "ee," it is always written as "ei."

For example,

foreign	neigh	freight
sleight	weigh	weight
height	reign	reins
leisure	reindeer	feint

Plurals

✳ Rule 14

a. To form the plural of most nouns we just add an "s."

For example,

biscuits	theaters	cows	dogs
horses	committees	cats	bridges
bicycles	adults	cakes	solutions

b. Words ending in "ful" form the plural in the usual way, by adding an "s."

For example,

basketfuls	tinfuls	pocketfuls	spoonfuls
armfuls	spadefuls	bagfuls	
cupfuls	bucketfuls	handfuls	

✳ Rule 15

Add "es" to nouns that end in "ch," "sh," "o," "s," "x" and "z" to form the plural.

For example,

class – classes	lash – lashes	watch – watches	echo – echoes
arch – arches	fox – foxes	leash – leashes	box – boxes
atlas – atlases	potato – potatoes		

Exceptions are:

bamboo – bamboos	kangaroo – kangaroos	shampoo – shampoos
cockatoo – cockatoos	zoo – zoos	radio – radios
banjo – banjos	soprano – sopranos	merino – merinos
solo – solos	photo – photos	silo – silos
piano – pianos	zero – zeros	ratio – ratios
monarch – monarchs	stomach – stomachs	

We only add an "s" to monarch and stomach as the "ch" sound has a "k."

☀ Rule 16

When a noun ends in "f" or "fe" we change the "f" to "v" and add "es" to form the plural.

For example,

calf – calves	*life – lives*	*half – halves*	*wife – wives*
sheaf – sheaves	*knife – knives*	*thief – thieves*	*wolf – wolves*
self – selves	*yourself – yourselves*	*shelf – shelves*	*elf – elves*

Note:

Either wharfs or wharves and hoofs or hooves are acceptable.

Exceptions are:

reefs	*roofs*	*waifs*	*puffs*
sheriffs	*staffs*	*stuffs*	*skiffs*
handkerchiefs	*gulfs*	*cliffs*	*chiefs*

☀ Rule 17

Many nouns form their plural by changing their vowel or vowels.

For example,

man – men	*oasis – oases*
woman – women	*crisis – crises*
tooth – teeth	*axis – axes*
goose – geese	*basis – bases*
foot – feet	*emphasis – emphases*
parenthesis – parentheses	

Exceptions are:

human – humans

Rule 18

Some nouns have no singular form.

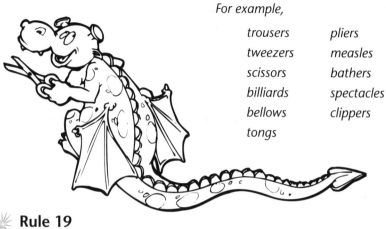

For example,

trousers	pliers
tweezers	measles
scissors	bathers
billiards	spectacles
bellows	clippers
tongs	

Rule 19

A few nouns have the same singular form as the plural form.

For example,

Singular	Plural
one cod	many cod
one dozen	many dozen
one gallows	many gallows
one deer	many deer
one salmon	many salmon
one sheep	many sheep
one trout	many trout
one score	many score
one swine	many swine
one reindeer	many reindeer

Rule 20

Most compound nouns form the plural by making the principal word of the compound noun plural.

For example,

passer-by	*passers-by*	*son-in-law*	*sons-in-law*
daughter-in-law	*daughters-in-law*	*sister-in-law*	*sisters-in-law*
brother-in-law	*brothers-in-law*	*maid-of-honor*	*maids-of-honor*

Rule 21

a. In English we often use the plural form of Latin words.

For example,
radius – radii
fungus – fungi
terminus – termini
cactus – cacti

b. Some English words have foreign origins so watch their plural.

For example,
datum – data
phenomenon – phenomena
erratum – errata
larva – larvae

☀ Rule 22

a. To form the past tense of some verbs we add "ed" or "d" where the word ends with "e."

For example,

lace – laced	*trace – traced*	*escape – escaped*	*walk – walked*
laugh – laughed	*talk – talked*	*wash – washed*	*wish – wished*

b. Some verbs that have a single vowel sound followed by a single consonant double the last letter before adding "ed."

For example,

wrap – wrapped	*strap – strapped*	*flap – flapped*	*trap – trapped*
fit – fitted	*plod – plodded*	*bug – bugged*	*pin – pinned*

☀ Rule 23

"t" is used instead of "ed" when writing the past tense of some words.

For example,

sweep – swept	*feel – felt*	*keep – kept*	*sleep – slept*
creep – crept	*weep – wept*	*spend – spent*	*kneel – knelt*
build – built	*lend – lent*		

☀ Rule 24

In some words, instead of adding "ed" for the past tense, a change is made in the spelling of the word.

For example,

lead – led	*shine – shone*	*lose – lost*	*tear – tore*
weave – wove	*run – ran*	*freeze – froze*	*shake – shook*
rise – rose	*think – thought*	*take – took*	*write – wrote*
buy – bought	*steal – stole*	*fight – fought*	*teach – taught*

✳ Rule 25

The general rule concerning a prefix is simply to add it.

For example,

un/certain	*un/numbered*	*dis/satisfied*	*up/roar*
dis/approve	*up/set*	*dis/solve*	*un/sure*
un/just	*re/view*	*mis/take*	*re/appear*

Prefix	Meaning	Examples
after–	following, behind	afternoon, afterwards
ante–, anti–	before in time	antebellum, ante meridiem
ant–, anti–	against	antiaircraft, antivenom
auto–	self	autobiography, autograph
be–	to make or do all over, by, near to	befriend, beside
bene–	well	beneficial, benefactor
bi–, bin–, bis–	two, twice	biannual, bicycle
centi–	one hundredth	centimeter
circum–	about, around	circumference
contra–, counter–	against, opposite	contradict, counteract
de–	away from, reversal, separation, negation	descend, deject, defend
deca–, deka–	ten times greater	decade, decagon
deci–	one tenth	deciliter
di–, dis–	two, twice	dissect, dialogue
en–, em–	to make, in, into, on	embark, encase
equi–	equal	equidistant
ex–	former, out of	exchange, excellence
extra–	beyond, outside	extraordinary
for–	denial, from, away	forbid, forgiven

Prefix	Meaning	Examples
fore–	before, front	forearm, forewarn
hecto–	100 times greater	hectare
hemi–	half	hemisphere
hexa–	six	hexagonal
hetero–	different, other	heterogeneous
homo–	same	homophone
hydro–	water	hydroelectric, hydrofoil
hyper–	above, over	hyperactive, hypersensitive
hypo–	less than, under	hypoactive, hypocrite
ig–, il–, im–, in–, ir–	not, opposite of	illegal, import, insane, irregular
im–, in–	in, into, to make	import, indoors, inland
inter–	among, between	interview, interrupt
intro–	inwardly, within	introvert
kilo–	1,000 times greater	kilogram
macro–	long, large	macropedia
magni–	large, great	magnification
micro–	one millionth, very small	microscope, microliter
mid–	in the middle of	midair, midday
milli–	one thousandth	millimeter
mis–	bad, wrong, fault	mishap, misbehave
mono–	one, above, single	monoplane, monocle
multi–	many	multicultural, multipurpose
non–	against, not, exclusion, negation	nonsense, non-attendance
o–, ob–, oc–, of–, op–	in the way of, against	obstruct, occur, oppress
omni–	all	omnivore

Prefixes

Prefix	Meaning	Examples
out–	beyond	outback, outboard, outfield
over–	above, beyond	overcast, overact, overcoat
par–, para–	beside, near, beyond, aside, amiss	parallel, paraplegic
penta–	five	pentagon
peri–	around	perimeter
post–	after, behind	postdate, postnatal, postpone
pre–	before, prior to	prearrange, preface, predict
pro–	before	program
re–	back or again	recall, report, redo
retro–	backwards	retrograde, retrospect
self–	reflexive action	self-control, self-absorbed
semi–	half	semicircle, semitone
sub–	under, below	submarine, submerge
super–	above, over	superhuman, superior
to–	this	today, tonight
trans–	across, beyond	transfer, transmit
tri–	three	triangle, tripod
twi–	double	twice, twin
ultra–	excessively	ultraconservative, ultrasensitive
un–	not, opposite, reverse	unable, unclean, undone
under–	beneath, below	underworld, undercurrent
up–	upwards	uphill, uplift, upright
with–	from, against, back	withhold, withstand

Rule 26

The general rule concerning a suffix is simply to add it.

For example,

play – play/s – play/ed – play/er – play/ing – play/ful
work – work/s – work/ed – work/er – work/ing – work/able
help – help/s – help/ed – help/er – help/ing – help/ful

Suffix	Meaning	Examples
–able, –ible, –uble	capable of	audible, edible, soluble
–age	collectivity	coinage
–al, –an, –ar	having the nature of	Australian, floral, solar
–an	of, having to do with	historian, politician, electrician
–ance, –ence	state of being, action	appearance, confidence
–ant, –ent	having quality of	ignorant, vibrant
–ant, –ar, –er, –or	one who, that which	assistant, confidant, actor, teacher
–arium, –orium, –ery, –ary, –ory	place for, place where act happens	aquarium, dictionary, territory
–ate, –en, –n, –ise	to make, become, cause, do	advertise, darken
–dom	state, condition, domain	kingdom, wisdom
–ed	past tense, furnished with, having	talked, gifted
–ee, –ent	one who	employee, student
–eer	one concerned with	mountaineer, buccaneer
–en, –et, –kin, –ling, –ock	small, little	duckling, piglet, floweret
–eous, –ous	full of, marked by	courteous, famous
–er	comparative degree	colder, faster, hotter, smaller
–ern	denotes direction	Northern, Western
–ese	originating from	Japanese, Burmese
–ess, –ress	feminine form	lioness, princess

Suffixes

Suffix	Meaning	Examples
–est	superlative degree	greatest, largest, slowest
–ette	diminutive, feminine	diskette, usherette
–ey, –y	like, nature of	dirty, sandy, smelly
–ful	full of, filled	cupful, beautiful, graceful
–fy	to make	justify, magnify
–hood, –ness, –ment, –t, –th	state of, condition	manhood, wilderness, argument
–ic	belonging to	athletic, poetic, public
–ing	continuous action	running, walking, talking
–ish	quality, belonging to	British, childish, foolish
–ism	state of being, action	heroism, activism
–ist	concerned with	biologist, geologist
–ity, –ety	condition, quality	naivety, stupidity
–ive	relating to, able to	native, supportive
–less	without	lifeless, colorless
–let	small, little	droplet, pamphlet
–like	similar to	childlike, wormlike
–ly	like, manner	clumsily, loudly, sadly
–ship	rank, state of being	lordship, friendship
–some	tendency, quality	handsome, lonesome
–teen, –ty	ten	fourteen, forty
–ward, –wards	direction	eastward, forward, downward
–way, –ways	manner	anyway, always
–wise	direction of, manner	lengthwise, likewise
–y, –ty	state of being	poverty, wealthy, healthy

Rule 27

When words end in "ac" or "ic"
always add "k" before adding the
suffixes "y," "ed," "er" and "ing."

For example,

frolic – frolicked – frolicking
mimic – mimicked – mimicking
traffic – trafficked – trafficking
picnic – picnicked – picnicking – picnicker
panic – panicked – panicking – panicky
colic – colicky

Rule 28

In the whole of the English language, only one word ends in
"icly." That word is "publicly." To all other words ending in
"ic," "ally" is added.

For example,

sarcastically	*tragically*
emphatically	*romantically*
problematically	*mathematically*
magically	*heroically*
economically	*socially*

Rule 29

This is a very important rule for adding a suffix. It is called the one, one, one rule.

When adding a suffix beginning with a vowel ("y," "ed," "er," "est," or "ing") to words of one syllable which have one short vowel followed by one consonant, always double the consonant before adding the suffix. This is done to keep the short vowel.

For example,

plan – planned – planner – planning   *hop – hopped – hopper – hopping*
stop – stopped – stopper – stopping   *skip – skipped – skipper – skipping*
thin – thinner – thinnest – thinning   *fat – fatter – fattest – fatty*

Exceptions are:

bus, gas and words that end in "w"

Rule 30

No consonant is doubled after a long vowel or a double vowel.

a.   *Long vowel examples,*

   wave – waved – waving   *bake – baked – baker – baking*
   love – loves – loved – loving   *smile – smiles – smiled – smiling*
   use – user – used – using   *blaze – blazer – blazed – blazing*

b.   *Double vowel examples,*

   clean – cleaned – cleaner – cleanest   *trail – trailed – trailer – trailing*
   cheer – cheered – cheering – cheerful   *train – trained – trainer – training*
   play – played – player – playing   *float – floated – floater – floating*

c.   *When two consonants follow a short vowel, no letter is doubled.*

   print – printed – printer – printing   *walk – walked – walker – walking*
   bank – banked – banker – banking   *talk – talked – talker – talking*
   farm – farmed – farmer – farming
   crush – crushed – crusher – crushing

✳ Rule 31

With words of more than one syllable we can still use the one,
one, one rule providing the consonant follows a single vowel.

For example,

re/fit – re/fit/ted – re/fit/ting
re/fer – re/fer/red – re/fer/ring
un/pin – un/pin/ned – un/pin/ning
out/run – out/run/ning
ad/mit – ad/mit/ted – ad/mit/ting
pre/fer – pre/fer/red – pre/fer/ring
kid/nap – kid/nap/ped – kid/nap/ping

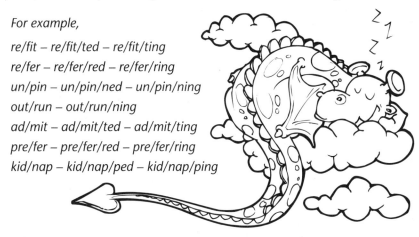

✳ Rule 32

When adding a suffix beginning with a consonant to a word
ending in the silent "e," always retain the silent "e" to keep the
long vowel long.

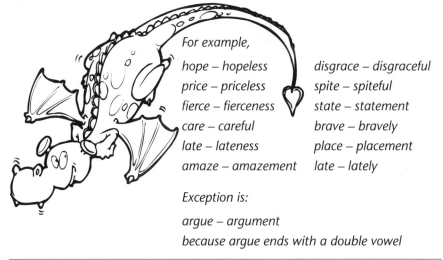

For example,

hope – hopeless	*disgrace – disgraceful*
price – priceless	*spite – spiteful*
fierce – fierceness	*state – statement*
care – careful	*brave – bravely*
late – lateness	*place – placement*
amaze – amazement	*late – lately*

Exception is:

argue – argument
because argue ends with a double vowel

Rule 33

When adding a suffix beginning with a vowel to a word ending in the silent "e," always drop the "e" as the vowel does the work of the silent "e."

For example,

hope – hoping	lace – laced
advise – advised	like – likable
argue – arguable	arrive – arriving
manage – managed	come – coming
glue – gluing	move – moved
argue – arguing	write – writing
place – placing	style – stylish
please – pleasing	wave – waving

So Stylish!

Exceptions are:

a. *Words ending in double "e" (ee) always keep the "ee" when adding the suffix "ing."*

For example,

referee – refereeing
see – seeing
guarantee – guaranteeing
flee – fleeing
disagree – disagreeing

b. *Always retain the silent "e" when adding "ing" to these words.*

canoe – canoeing	shoe – shoeing	hoe – hoeing
dye – dyeing	toe – toeing	singe – singeing
tiptoe – tiptoeing	eye – eyeing	

✳ Rule 34

a. When adding a suffix beginning with an "a," as in "able," after a soft "c" or "g," always retain the silent "e" to keep the "c" or "g" soft.

For example,

traceable	*replaceable*	*peaceable*
noticeable	*enforceable*	*manageable*
serviceable	*chargeable*	*changeable*

b. When a suffix begins with an "o" we retain the silent "e" to keep the "g" soft.

For example,

outrage – outrageous   courage – courageous
advantage – advantageous

✳ Rule 35

a. When adding "ous" to words ending in "ce" we change the "e" to "i" before adding "ous."

For example,

grace – gracious   space – spacious   avarice – avaricious

b. When the suffix begins with an "i" after the soft "ce" or "ge" always drop the silent "e" as the "i" will keep the "c" or "g" soft.

For example,

manage – managing	*notice – noticing*
race – racing	*encourage – encouraging*
enforce – enforcing	*trace – tracing*
exchange – exchanging	*interchange – interchanging*
service – servicing	*charge – charging*

Exception is: singe – singeing

Suffixes

✳ Rule 36

When adding a "y" to a word ending in "e," drop the "e" before adding the "y."

For example,

ease – easy	craze – crazy	smoke – smoky	rose – rosy
haze – hazy	breeze – breezy	juice – juicy	laze – lazy
ice – icy	noise – noisy	lace – lacy	nose – nosy
stone – stony	edge – edgy	wire – wiry	

✳ Rule 37

a. To add "ly" to words ending in "e," after a consonant just change the "e" to "y."

For example,

horrible – horribly	visible – visibly	probable – probably
noble – nobly	noticeable – noticeably	subtle – subtly
forcible – forcibly	feeble – feebly	terrible – terribly
simple – simply	comfortable – comfortably	idle – idly

b. When adding "ly" to a word ending in "le" after a vowel, just write "ly" after the "le."

For example,

vile – vilely	futile – futilely	sole – solely
pale – palely	versatile – versatilely	juvenile – juvenilely

Exceptions are:

whole – wholly

Rule 38

The silent "e" is retained before "ly" and "ty" to keep the long vowel long.

For example,

lovely	*rudely*	*bravely*	*surely*
largely	*princely*	*lonely*	*strangely*
homely	*nicely*	*safety*	*ninety*

Exceptions are:

true – truly   *due – duly*
because they end in a double vowel.

Rule 39

a. When the final "y" in any word is preceded by a vowel we retain the "y" when adding a suffix.

For example,

day – days

donkey – donkeys

say – says – saying

pay – pays – paying

buoy – buoys – buoyed – buoying – buoyant – buoyancy

survey – surveys – surveyor – surveyed – surveying

play – plays – played – player – playing

pray – prays – prayer – praying – prayed

boy – boys

ray – rays

relay – relays – relayed

Exceptions are:

say – said   *day – daily*   *pay – paid*

b. Always keep the "y" when adding the suffix "ing" or any other suffix beginning with an "i," because in the English language we seldom write "ii."

For example,

marrying	*relying*	*copying*	*carrying*
occupying	*hobbyist*	*tidying*	*boyish*
defying	*babyish*		

Exceptions are:

skiing   *taxiing*

c. When adding a suffix beginning with a vowel or a consonant to a word ending in "y," change the "y" to "i" before adding the suffix.

For example,

| *silky – silkiest* | *pity – pitiful* | *marry – marries* | *army – armies* |
| *busy – busier* | *hurry – hurried* | *heavy – heavier* | *pretty – prettiest* |

Rule 40

With words ending in "our" and
"ous," omit the "u" before adding
"ous" or "ity."

For example,

glamour – glamorous   *curious – curiosity*
generous – generosity   *monstrous – monstrosity*

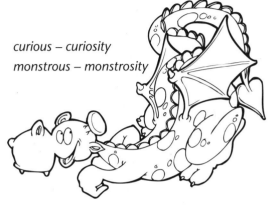

Rule 41

In the English language there are only three words made by
adding the suffix "ceed." They are:

exceed   proceed   succeed

Only one English word is spelled with "sede." That is:

supersede

All other words end in "cede."

For example,

intercede   *recede*
precede   *secede*
accede   *concede*

Suffixes

✳ Rule 42

a. Words ending in "ant" we change to "ance" in the noun form.

For example,

abundant – abundance	*ignorant – ignorance*	*entrant – entrance*
tolerant – tolerance	*assistant – assistance*	*defiant – defiance*
elegant – elegance	*extravagant – extravagance*	*distant – distance*

b. Some words ending in "ent" change to "ence" in the noun form.

For example,

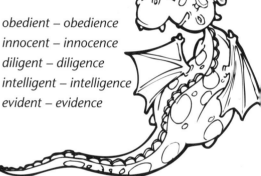

dependent – dependence	*obedient – obedience*
silent – silence	*innocent – innocence*
resident – residence	*diligent – diligence*
present – presence	*intelligent – intelligence*
absent – absence	*evident – evidence*

✳ Rule 43

When changing some adjectives to the noun form, we add "th."

For example,

wide – width	*grow – growth*	*eight – eighth*
six – sixth	*warm – warmth*	*four – fourth*
seven – seventh	*nine – ninth*	

Note: Most numbers form the noun by adding "th."

Exceptions are:

first, second and third in all family groups; for example, twenty-first, thirty-second, forty-third.

Rule 44

There are two main uses for apostrophes. One is to show when a letter or letters have been omitted.

For example,

could not – couldn't   *has not – hasn't*
did not – didn't   *I am – I'm*
you will – you'll   *were not – weren't*
cannot – can't   *will not – won't*
I will – I'll   *had not – hadn't*
we are – we're   *I would – I'd*
you are – you're   *she is – she's*
he had – he'd   *it is – it's*
they are – they're   *who is – who's*

Note: The words ours, yours, hers and theirs never have an apostrophe.

Apostrophes

☀ **Rule 45**

The other use of an apostrophe is to show ownership.

The sentence: The tail of the cat was fluffy.   *can be written*
                The cat's tail was fluffy.

a. To single nouns we add an apostrophe before the "s" to show ownership or the possessive form of the noun.

For example,

The shoes of the dancer.	*The dancer's shoes.*
The brooch belonging to Mother.	*Mother's brooch.*
The tail of the dog.	*The dog's tail.*
The life of the man.	*The man's life.*
The book of a prince.	*The prince's book.*
The house of the mayor.	*The mayor's house.*
The petals of a flower.	*The flower's petals.*

b. When some singular nouns end in "s," the rule still applies. Another "s" is added after the apostrophe.

For example,

The class's interest was aroused.
The moss's texture was soft.
The lass's blue eyes sparkled.
The princess's jewels shone brightly.

c. To some proper nouns ending in "s" we still apply the rule when writing the possessive form.

For example,

Mrs. Jones's house.	*Mr. Moss's speech.*
Frank Sim's book.	*James's hat.*
Mrs. Pinkus's cat.	*Judy Nicholas's success.*

Rule 45 cont.

d. When a proper noun ending in "s" is preceded by a "z" sound, it is usual not to add an "s" after the apostrophe but just add an apostrophe.

For example,

The teachings of Jesus – Jesus' teachings.
The laws of Moses – Moses' laws.

Some long classical names would sound awkward if another "s" was added, so we just add an apostrophe.

For example,

Aristophanes' comedies.   *Alcibiades' treachery.*
Euripides' tragedies.   *Archimedes' principle.*

e. Measurement of size, weight, time and space may be used possessively and take an apostrophe "s" in the usual way.

For example,

a dollar's worth
a week's vacation
an hour's delay
a pin's point
a hair's breadth
a year's leave

f. When such measurements are plural, we just add an apostrophe after the "s."

For example,

three dollars' worth   *two weeks' vacation*
four hours' delay   *three years' leave*

Apostrophes

✳ Rule 45 cont.

g. Most plural nouns already end in "s," so to write the possessive form of the noun, we just add an apostrophe after the "s."

For example,

The girls' new dresses.
The farmers' crops.
The boys' laughter.
The two dogs' tails.
The babies' bottles.

Note:

Some plural nouns do not end in "s."

For example,

| *people* | *men* | *women* | *children* | *oxen* |

These words are treated the same way as the singular form of the noun when writing the possessive form.

For example,

people's opinion
children's toys
women's hats
oxen's load
men's shoes

These are gimmicks that help us to spell certain words.

1. The "ui" words.
   These are good-mannered words, as "u" comes before "i."

   For example,

   You and I will eat some fruit.
   You and I will wear a suit.
   You and I will wear suitable shoes.
   You and I will build a house.
   You and I know Mr. Jones, the builder.
   You and I belong to the worker's guild.
   You and I are Girl Guides.

2. Waist and waste.
   Remember: **I** have a wa**i**st but it is wast**e** pap**e**r.

3. Pursue means to run after.
   Both p**u**rs**u**e and r**u**n are spelled with a "u."

4. Persuade and person.
   We sometimes have to **per**suade a **per**son.

5. Here, there and where.
   These all mean a place and all are spelled with "here" in them.

   For example,

   ***Here** is a place to stay.*
   ***There** is the place I told you about.*
   ***Where** is the place you just mentioned?*

6. Hear and heard.
   Any word meaning to hear something has "ear" in it.

   For example,

   I *hear* a sound.
   I *heard* a sound.

7. Loose and lose.
   To tell the difference between lose and loose, remember:
   Loose has two o's as in **loo**se t**oo**th.

8. Forest.
   The word tree has only one "r," so has the word forest only one "r."

9. Principal and principle.
   The princi**pal** is my **pal**.

10. Stationery and stationary.
    Stationery is writing paper and pens.
    A stationary car is still.

11. Currant and current.
    Currants are found in cakes.
    The river has many currents.

Homophones are words that sound the same but are spelled differently. They often cause spelling errors.

aisle	The bride walked down the **aisle** of the church.
isle	The **Isle** of Man.
altar	The priest knelt at the **altar**.
alter	Do not **alter** your answer.
aloud	Say it **aloud**.
allowed	We are **allowed** to go to the park.
ate	I **ate** a large breakfast.
eight	It is **eight** o'clock in the evening.
border	The **border** of the states is very remote.
boarder	I am a **boarder** at St. Hilda's school.
barren	This land is **barren**.
baron	The **baron** was in his castle.
berry	The black**berry** jam was tasty.
bury	**Bury** the roots of the plant carefully.
birth	My **birth**day is December 14th.
berth	The ship will **berth** at that wharf.
bare	The cupboard was **bare**.
bear	The large, white **bear** was very angry.
brake	The **brake**s of the car failed.
break	Be careful not to **break** the glass.
chews	The cow **chews** her cud.
choose	Please **choose** the one you like the most.
course	That is the local golf **course**.
coarse	This is very **coarse** material.

Homophones

currant	Grapes turn into **currant**s.
current	The river **current** is dangerous.
corps	The Army **Corps** was camped nearby.
core	The **core** of the apple was lost.
council	The Shire **Council** raised the land rates.
counsel	The social worker will **counsel** her.
cereal	**Cereal** is good for breakfast.
serial	I read that story as a **serial**.
complement	The ship has a full **complement** of men.
compliment	I must **compliment** you on your excellent work.
ceiling	The lounge room **ceiling** needs painting.
sealing	Use the **sealing** wax to seal the wood.
dyeing	They were **dyeing** the wool black.
dying	The flowers were **dying** in the vase.
desert	The **desert** is a dry and sandy track of land.
desert	To **desert** your friend would be unfair.
dessert	The **dessert** is generally the final course of a meal.
foul	That was a **foul** trick you played on your brother.
fowl	That **fowl** is for Thanksgiving dinner.

faint	I feel quite **faint**.
feint	The general made a **feint** to confuse his enemy.
gate	Please close the **gate**.
gait	The gorilla had a peculiar **gait**.
guest	Mary is our special **guest**.
guessed	You have **guessed** the answer correctly.
hole	The **hole** in my shoe is getting larger.
whole	He ate the **whole** loaf.
horse	He is a champion **horse**.
hoarse	My voice is **hoarse** today.
hale	He is **hale** and hearty.
hail	The **hail** damaged the fruit on the trees.
idle	That boy is always **idle**.
idol	Elvis Presley was my **idol**.
know	Do you **know** the answer?
no	**No**, I won't lend you my pen.
knew	I **knew** the answer all the time.
new	That is a lovely **new** dress.
key	I have lost my **key**.
quay	The ship will berth at the **quay**.
knead	The baker will **knead** the dough.
need	I **need** a new pair of jeans.
led	The champion **led** all the way.
lead	Water pipes were made of **lead**.

Homophones

load	That **load** is too heavy to carry.
lode	A **lode** is a vein of metallic ore.
main	That is the **main** road.
mane	They cut the horse's **mane**.
medal	He won a **medal** for running.
meddle	Do not **meddle** in other people's affairs.
mettle	The horse showed his true **mettle**.
metal	**Metal** will rust if left outside unprotected.
maid	The house**maid** left us in the lurch.
made	He carefully designed and **made** a bird cage.
praise	The teacher will always **praise** good work.
preys	The eagle **preys** on rabbits for its food.
prays	A Christian **prays** to God.
plain	The cattle roam on the **plain**.
plane	The **plane** made a crash landing.
piece	Please pass me that **piece** of paper.
peace	**Peace** is better than war.
paws	The cat likes to lick her **paws**.
pause	The **pause** button on the recorder can be used when you need to take a break.
profits	All **profits** were given to charity.
prophets	Some **prophets** can tell the future.

rap	**Rap** on the door loudly.
wrap	**Wrap** the present carefully.
right	Please check if your answer is **right**.
write	Please **write** neatly in your pad.
rose	The **rose** plant is in full bloom.
rows	There were **rows** and **rows** of seats.
rote	You must learn your tables by **rote**.
wrote	He **wrote** me a long letter.
steel	A roof beam is made of **steel**.
steal	To **steal** is a criminal offense.
site	They have chosen the **site** for the new school.
sight	That poor man has lost his **sight**.
strait	We sailed down Bass **Strait**.
straight	Draw a **straight** line from A to B.
sow	You must **sow** the seed evenly.
sew	Please **sew** the seam of the skirt neatly.
stairs	These **stairs** are not safe.
stares	He **stares** at people who are passing by.
stationary	The car was **stationary** on the side of the road.
stationery	Writing pad and envelopes are classified as **stationery**.
sent	I have **sent** the birthday card to my friend.
scent	The **scent** of the bear was obvious.

Homophones

seen	He was **seen** leaving the house.
scene	Act 1, **Scene** 2.
to	We are going **to** school.
too	You are **too** heavy to carry.
two	**Two** is company, three is a crowd.
throne	Queen Elizabeth occupies the **throne**.
thrown	He has **thrown** away his apple.
threw	I **threw** my rubbish in the bin.
through	Go **through** the front door.

vane	The weather **vane** moves with the direction of the wind.
vein	**Vein**s carry blood back to the heart.
vain	Their hard work was all in **vain**.
wave	That was a large **wave**.
waive	I will **waive** my claim to the money.
weather	The **weather** has been mild this year.
whether	I don't know **whether** we will be able to play outside.
wear	I will **wear** my new dress.
ware	What type of **ware**s are you selling?
where	**Where** is your older brother?

waste	Do not **waste** that good paper.
waist	My **waist** is becoming too large.
weighed	The jockey **weighed** his saddle.
wade	Do not **wade** in the large puddle.
wait	Please **wait** here.
weight	What **weight** are you?
yolk	The **yolk** of the egg was deep yellow.
yoke	A **yoke** is a wooden neck piece used by oxen when pulling a heavy load.

Homographs

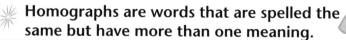

Homographs are words that are spelled the same but have more than one meaning.

angle	column	game	lock	private	spring
arms	corn	grain	log	prune	squash
back	count	grate	mail	pupil	staff
ball	court	grave	march	race	stage
bank	craft	ground	mass	range	stall
bar	crane	gum	master	rank	stand
bark	cricket	hail	match	record	star
base	crop	hamper	may	reflect	state
bat	cross	hand	mean	rent	steer
bay	crow	hide	might	rest	stern
beam	dam	hit	mine	rifle	stick
bear	dart	hold	mint	right	stock
beat	dear	host	mold	ring	stole
bill	deck	iron	mount	rock	strike
bit	dock	jam	nail	roll	stud
blade	down	jar	nature	rose	stump
blind	draft	jet	note	round	suit
block	draw	joint	order	row	swallow
blow	drill	jumper	organ	ruler	swift
bluff	drive	just	page	rung	table
board	drone	kid	palm	sack	tear
boot	duck	kind	pass	safe	temper
bow	express	kite	patient	sand	tile
brand	fair	lap	peal	save	till
calf	fast	last	pen	scale/s	top
cape	felt	lawn	pick	seal	train
capital	file	lay	pine	season	trip
carpet	fill	lead	pipe	shed	tumbler
case	fine	lean	pitch	sheet	turn
cashier	fire	leaves	plane	sign	wake
cast	firm	left	plant	sink	watch
change	fit	let	play	soil	wave
charge	flag	letter	plot	sound	well
chop	fleet	lie	plug	sow	wind
club	float	lift	pole	speaker	work
coach	fold	light	port	spell	yard
coast	foot	line	post	spoke	
coat	forge	list	pound		
cold	form	litter	power		

Root Words

Root words are parts of words which originated in another language. They have been used in the English language to form the base of some words we use.

Root	Meaning	Root	Meaning
acro–	top	crypto–	hidden
aeq.	equal	crystallo–	crystal
aero	air	cursus	running
alter	other	cycl–	cycle
alto	high	cyto–	cell
amor	love	cyst–	cyst
amphi–	on all sides	–cyte	cell
–androus	male	deca–	ten
anima	breath, life	demo–	people
aniso–	unlike	demon–	demon
anthropo–	human	denti–	tooth
apia	bee	–derm	skin
aqua	water	ducere	to lead
audio–	hear	duo–	two
auto–	self	dys–	bad
avi–	bird	equi	equal
baro–	weight	endo–	within, inside
bene–	good, well	entero–	intestine
bi	twice	ethno–	race, tribe
biblio	book	factor	do
bio	life	fertilis	to make fruitful
brevi–	short	finis	end
cardio–	heart	fluor	flow
capere	to take hold	gastro–	stomach
caput	head	geo–	earth
centum	hundred	–gerous	producing
–chrome	color	–gram	letter, writing
chrono–	time	–graph	write
–cide	killer	–gyno	woman
circum–	around	–gyro–	circle
civis	citizen	hetero–	other
–claudere	shut, close	holo–	whole
cor	heart	homo–	same
cosmeo	world	ideo–	idea
counter–	against	manus	hand
cranium–	skull	mille	thousand
credo	I believe	mini–	small

Root Words

Root	Meaning	Root	Meaning
minuere	to lessen	photo–	light
mittere	to send	physio–	physical
mono–	one, alone	phyto–	plant
–morph	form	–plasty	formation
mors	death	poly–	many
movere	move	portare	carry, bear
multi–	many	prima	first
my–	muscle	project	throw
myc–	fungus	proto–	first
myth–	myth	pseudo–	false
myx–	slimy	psych–	mind
natus	born	ptero–	wing
navis	ship	pyo–	pus
nector	dead	quadri–	four
neo–	new	quinque–	five
nepho–	cloud	recti–	set upright
nephro–	kidney	scrib	write
nocti–	night	–sect	cut
novem	nine	septum	seven
octa	eight	sex–	six
omni–	all	Sino–	Chinese
ortho–	straight, right	spectro–	look
paed–	child	–sphere	sphere
pan–	all	spiro–	spiral
patho–	suffering	–stat	stationary
pedis	foot	statua	statue
pendere	hang	tele–	afar, end
penta–	five	terra	earth
–phasia	disordered speech	tractum	trace
phen	used in chemistry	tetra	four
–philia	lover of	tri–	three
phlebo–	vein	twi–	two, twice
–phobia	fear	uni–	one
phon–	sound, voice	video	see
–phorous	bearing, having	vox	voice
phosp–	phosphorous		

☀ Capital letters are used:

1. To begin a sentence.

   For example,

   The dog likes to chase cats down the street.
   My pet fish is blue and orange.
   When are we going to the beach?

2. For proper nouns.

   For example,

   Names of people – Ted Harris, Mrs. Sanders
   Names of places – Boston, Paris, Maritime Museum
   Names of streets – Redwood Crescent, Floreat Boulevard
   To begin important words in the titles of books, songs, etc. – Huckleberry Finn, Red Riding Hood
   Days of the week – Monday, Sunday
   Months of the year – April, November
   Gods and Goddesses – Venus, Hercules, Aphrodite
   Names of planets – Mars, Mercury, Saturn

3. For adjectives derived from proper nouns.

   For example,

   American
   English
   Japanese
   Indonesian

4. For the pronoun "I."

   For example,

   My brother and I walked to school on Tuesday.

Abbreviations

✳ **An abbreviation is a word that has been shortened by leaving out some of the letters.**

For example,

Dr. – Doctor
govt. – government
pop. – population
St. – street or saint

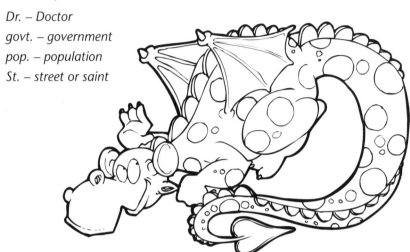

1. When an abbreviation does not include the last letter of the full word, a period is generally added after the abbreviation.

For example,

abbrev. – abbreviation
approx. – approximately
e.g. – for example
fol. – following
lat. – latitude
tbsp. – tablespoon
tsp. – teaspoon
Apr. – April
Wed. – Wednesday

Exceptions are:

dept. – the first "t" is counted, not the final "t"

2. Abbreviations which consist of more than one capital letter, or capital letters only, do not generally require periods.

For example,

USA – United States of America
DOB – Date of Birth
PO – Post Office
HO – Head Office
MP – Military Police
NY – New York
UN – United Nations

3. Abbreviations of units of measurement do not need a period.

For example,
cm – centimeter
g – gram
kg – kilogram
km – kilometer
mm – millimeter
L – liter
m – meter
mL – milliliter

Acronyms

An acronym is a word made up from the letters of other words.

1. They are usually formed from the first letters.

   For example,

   *AIDS – **a**cquired **i**mmune **d**eficiency **s**yndrome*
   *Basic – **B**eginners' **A**ll-purpose **S**ymbolic **I**nstruction **C**ode*
   *Laser – **L**ight **A**mplification by **S**timulated **E**mission of **R**adiation*
   *Qantas – **Q**ueensland **an**d **N**orthern **T**erritory **A**erial **S**ervices*
   *Scuba – **S**elf-**c**ontained **U**nderwater **B**reathing **A**pparatus*
   *WHO – **W**orld **H**ealth **O**rganization*

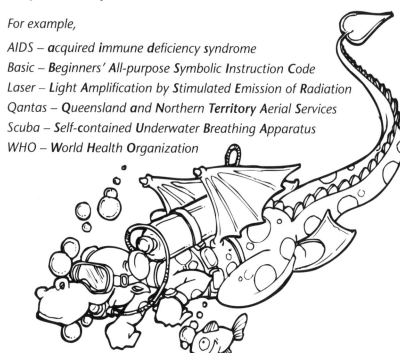

2. They may also be formed from a number of letters.

   For example,

   *radar – **ra**dio **d**etection **a**nd **r**anging*
   *sitcom – **sit**uation **com**edy*
   *sonar – **so**und, **na**vigation and **r**anging*

3. Acronyms are written without periods.

Eponyms are words that have originated from people's names or the names of places.

ampere – French physicist

banksia – English naturalist

bowie – American soldier

boycott – Irish land agent

braille – French teacher

caesarean – Roman general

cardigan – English earl

diesel – German engineer

dunce – English scholar

Ferris wheel – American engineer

gerrymander – American governor

guillotine – French physician

guy – Leader, English Gunpowder Plot

Hansard – English printer

hooligan – English family who had a reputation for fighting

leotard – French acrobat

Levis – American manufacturer

lynch – American captain

mackintosh – Scottish inventor

maverick – American cattle raiser

Melba toast – Australian soprano

mesmerize – Austrian physician

morse code – American inventor

nicotine – French ambassador

pasteurize – French chemist

raglan – British commander

sandwich – British naval administrator

saxophone – Belgian instrument-maker

silhouette – French politician

spoonerism – English scholar

stroganoff – Russian diplomat

teddy bear – American President

tomfoolery – English fool

valentine – Roman saint

Victorian – English Queen

volts – Italian physicist

wellingtons – Wellington Duke

zeppelin – German designer

Anagrams

 Anagrams are new words formed from using all of the letters from another word in a different order.

able – bale

acme – came – mace

acre – care – race

act – cat

add – dad

aids – dais – said

ales – sale – seal

amble – blame

amen – mane – mean

ample – maple

ant – tan

are – ear – era

aril – lair – liar – rail

art – rat –tar

arts – rats – star

ash – has

asleep – elapse – please

astute – statue

ate – eat – tea

bad – dab

ban – nab

bat – tab

bats – stab

battle – tablet

bin – nib

bleat – table

blister – bristle

bog – gob

bowl – blow

brake – break

bruise – buries – rubies

bun – nub

bus – sub

but – tub

caned – dance

cares – scare

caret – trace

cars – scar

cater – crate

cedar – cared – raced

charm – march

claps – clasp – scalp

clean – lance

coins – icons – sonic

dale – deal – lade – lead

dam – mad

dare – dear – read

deer – reed

den – end

design – signed – singed

devil – lived

dew – wed

diet – tied

dim – mid

disease – seaside

dog – god

doom – mood

dust – stud

earth – heart

east – eats – seat – teas

edit – tide

emit – mite – time

enlarge – general

enlist – listen – silent – tinsel

evil – live – veil – vile

felt – left

file – life

filter – lifter – trifle

finger – fringe

flier – rifle

flow – fowl – wolf

fluster – restful

forest – foster – softer

groan – organ

gulp – plug

gut – tug

hoes – hose – shoe

hops – posh – shop

horse – shore

how – who

keep – peek

kiln – link

lame – male – meal

lamp – palm

lap – pal

leap – pale – peal – plea

least – stale – steal

lemon – melon

lemons – melons – solemn

liar – rail

limes – miles – slime – smile

loop – polo – pool

low – owl

lump – plum

luster – result – rustle

mantle – mental

marble – ramble

mate – meat – tame – team

meet – teem

moor – room

nails – slain

nap – pan

naps – pans – snap – span

nerve – never

net – ten

nip – pin

no – on

north – thorn

now – own – won

oils – soil

rose – sore

owe – woe

pals – slap

panel – plane

pare – pear – reap

part – tarp – trap

pat – tap

pate – peat – tape

paws – swap – wasp

petal – plate – pleat

petals – staple

pets – step

pins – spin

pit – tip

post – pots – spot –

stop – tops

pot – top

prides – spider

priest – sprite – stripe

raw – war

reins – resin – rinse –

risen – siren

reward – warder

rote – tore

same – seam

saw – was

serve – sever – verse

setter – street – tester

sinew – swine – wines

slate – tales

sleet – steel

spat – taps

state – taste

sword – words

tare – tear

Difficult Words to Spell

absence
academically
accelerate
accessible
accidentally
accommodation
achievement
acknowledge
acquaintance
acquire
across
adaptation
address
adequate
advertisement
aerial
agreeable
alcohol
allege
all right
a lot
already

altogether
amount
appalling
apparatus
apparently
appearance
appropriate
argument
article
associate
as well
attachment
attitude
author
awkward

bachelor
balloon
basically
beautiful
beginning
believe
benefited
bicycle
burglar
business

calendar
campaign
careful
carefully
category
caterpillar
cemetery

century
chaos
character
chief
circuit
collaborate
colleague
college
colonel
commission
committee
comparatively
comparison
competent
completely
conceive
concentrate
condemn
conjure
conscience
conscientious
conscious
consistent
conspiracy
contemporary
correspondence
courteous
criticism
cruelly
curiosity

deceit
decision
defense

defensive
definite
democracy
descendant
descent
description
despair
desperately
deteriorate
deterrent
developed
development
diarrhea
difference
dilemma
disappear
disappoint
disastrous
discipline
disobeyed
disservice
dissolve
duly

Difficult Words to Spell

ecstasy
eighth
elegant
embarrass
emperor
endeavor
enormous
environment
equatorial
estuary
exaggerate
exceed
excellent
except
exceptionally
excitement
exercise
exhibition
exhilarating
existence
expense
experience
extraordinary
extravagant
extremely

familiar
family
favorite
February
fiery
fluorescent
foreign
forfeit

fortunately
forty
fourteen
friend
fulfil
furniture

gauge
goddess
government
governor
grammar
grievous
guarantee
guard

handkerchief
harass
heaven
height
heir
horizon
humorous
humor
hygiene

identical
illegibly
immediately
imminent
infinite
innocence
inoculate
install

instalment/
  installment
intellectual
intelligence
interested
irrelevant
irreparable
irresistible

jealous
jewelry
justice

knowledgeable

laboratory
leisure
lieutenant
lightning
likelihood
literature
loneliness
maintain
maintenance
manageable
marriage
marvellous
mathematician
meant
medicine
medieval
Mediterranean
messenger
mimic

miniature
minute
miscellaneous
mischievous
murmured
mystify

naive
necessary
negotiate
neighbor
ninth
noon
noticeable
nuisance

occasionally
occurred
occurrence

Difficult Words to Spell

offered

opportunity

originally

paid

paralleled

paralyzed

parliamentary

particularly

pavilion

permanent

permissible

poisonous

possession

precede

preferred

prejudice

preparation

presence

primitive

privilege

probably

procedure

proceed

professor

pronunciation

proof

propeller

protrude

prove

psychiatrist

psychology

publicly

punctuation

pursue

quarter

queue

quietly

really

receipt

receive

recommend

referred

referee

reference

refrigerator

religious

repetition

reservoir

resistance

responsibility

restaurant

rhyme

rhythm

ridiculous

sandal

satellite

scary

scissors

secretary

seize

sentence

separate

silhouette

similarly

sincerely

skilful/skillful

soldier

solicitor

souvenir

speech

statistics

successfully

summarize

surprise

survivor

symmetry

technical

technique

temperature

temporary

tendency

terrifying

tomorrow

tongue

tragedy

tragic

tranquillity/
tranqulity

tries

truly

twelfth

tying

unnecessary

until

vacuum

valley

valuable

vegetable

vehicle

veterinary

vicious

vigorous

villain

virtually

weird

wholly

wield

wilful/willful

wiry

withhold

woolen

worshiped

yacht

Notes

Notes